I Quit

The Death of a Network Marketer

Dedicated to my wife and soul mate Peg
who never stopped believing in me.

By

Peter Wolfing

Table of Contents

Prologue

You see, million-dollar mindset is really just a Mind Game. You need to think differently.

You only get to make what you are as a person. Some of you reading this have made money very quickly in in Network Marketing.

If you don't quickly develop yourself as a person to catch up to the income, your income will come back down to where you are.

It doesn't matter how good the comp plan is. If you don't grow, your income will come down to where you are as a person.

It's been said that Network Marketing is personal development disguised as a business. I couldn't agree more.

You must quickly develop skills. You must quickly build new habits. You must quickly understand that you only get to make what you are.

You must break out of the "comfort zone" you are shackled by. It keeps you prisoner. You must stretch yourself every day like a rubber band. With the tension of the stretch come strength. You grow from this just as muscles grow when you work out. They grow due to the tension and stress put on them. That's what you need to do as a person. Stretch yourself. Increase the tension.

Rejection. Fail. Learn. Grow. Repeat the process only better. It's a simple process as old as time.

Most people just sleepwalk through life staying in their comfort zone. Their dream muscles deteriorate over time. It's called muscle atrophy. In layman's terms it's called "If you don't use it, you lose it." It's no different with dreams. It can be called "Dream Atrophy".

In order to break away from this common thinking, you need to think differently.

You can think like this...

"Everything is a scam."

"I'm too busy."

"The sponsor never returned my call."

"The company had a glitch."

"The products I ordered came in two days late."

"I have to take out the trash."

"My relatives said "Boo"! What makes you think you can do that "thing"."?

Yada. Yada. Yada.

You know why most wannabe network marketers fail to get a full-time income (or ANY income) from their actions? Because they seek to put the blame outwards, rather than inwards.

Think of this...

Every single big name success story (and I include myself in this) was where you are right now.

Burned. Scammed. Misled. Confused. Overwhelmed. Frustrated. Betrayed. Tired. (You add the words)

But you know what the successful people did different than most others?

They didn't quit. They didn't blame others. They didn't stop trying.

They accepted that they needed to learn the right process and work like a focused laser beam to implement that process.

 (And if you're not prepared to do that, stick to your day job - this is about building a business. It ain't gonna happen overnight and it takes time, money and sweat).

The moment you give in and say, "It's all someone else's fault" is the moment you've lost. The moment you're set free in this business is the moment you stop relying on your sponsor, the company or the magic system you may be in. So, you can read this and say; "Peter, that's easy for you to say from where you're standing."

OR...

You can read this and say;

"You know what Peter - you are dead right. I know I have everything in my power to turn this around."

And every single last successful network marketer on the face of this planet got there by doing the same thing;

Think Differently.

Learn from someone who's already achieved success.

Now I know if you're like most people - you can't afford thousands of dollars to be coached by me.

Which is one reason why I've written this book. It's a way for me to give you the Cliff Notes version of what stops most wannabes. I know because I've committed most of them. This book should be your conscience so when something happens that in written inside (and it will), you can ask yourself "I wonder what Peter said about that?".

This book allows anyone to be coached virtually and given easy-to-follow solutions to common problems that you can implement both quickly and easily. It shows you EXACTLY what you need to do to follow in my footsteps.

"I Quit" gives you the keys to the kingdom. It unlocks the vault of knowledge for you to take advantage of the hundreds of thousands of dollars I personally spent learning what I know. This book has it all condensed for you. Crazy I know but my mission having massive impact and to change as many lives as I can. "I Quit" is that way to effect and empower others to avoid some of the problems I ran into or get out of ones they're already in.

It's about thinking differently. It's fought in between your ears. It's not about recruiting, prospecting, learning the latest marketing tactic, communication skills or even your closing skills. It's about how you handle success and defeat. It's about getting up after you have been knocked down. It's about making a stand. This is the sign of a leader.

Your journey in Network Marketing is going to be a roller coaster ride.

One day you're on top of the world bringing in several new hot prospects that join your team and other days it's a grind where your marketing campaign might have not been as successful as you would have wanted. One day you're excited and other days you're disappointed questioning your very existence in this industry. All the while you are getting pounded by people trying to steal your dreams by them telling you to go and get a real JOB. You will start to question yourself. Can you do this? Can you make it happen? Is this the right business to been in?

The true war is in your mind.

Thinking differently says that Achievement is not about luck. It's more like a science.

Why should you trust what I say? Good question. When you have such a long and varied view of the industry both as a distributor and company owner, you have a unique perspective. Notice how I didn't mention all the money I have made. Because you could care less about what I make.

It's what I know that's important. If you have seen and experienced the ups and downs that I have, the underlying fundamental truths become crystal clear. The wisdom gained though going in debt over $100,000 twice as I invested in my business and education, the countless people I have spoken too, the teachings of masters of their craft that I have absorbed and implemented, the best practices of some of the industries greatest achievers, well, you can't help but learn a thing or two. The systems I have brought forth have worked for close to 2 decades. Hundreds of thousands of members have proven it.

I have gone through the gauntlet folks. If you have experienced any failures, the difference between you and I is that I have gone through more than you. I am no different than you other than I do more than most. It's not much more of a difficult concept as that.

Nobody can sell me on gimmicks. I have too many reference points. I just know what works.

As Jim Rohn said, "There are no new fundamentals. Truth is not new; it's old". You can choose to ignore it or embrace it.

Thinking differently is having a positive attitude during the slow time or hard times will be the key to your longevity. This can be done by understanding your "Why". Knowing why you started and needs to be a subliminal alarm clock for you when times get tough and they will get tough for you no matter how successful you think you are. Even the most successful money makers in this industry have off days, weeks, and months. There is No avoiding this. You cannot be perfect all the time.

Take the time to know your WHY. Make it a strong reason. Always forgive yourself for mishaps and understand that business has cycles. Forgive yourself for making mistakes.

Remember failure is success turn inside out.

With "I Quit, The Death of a Network Marketer" I want to give you the cure so you don't become a statistic.

Take your personal power back. I hope you enjoy this book and in some way, it has an impact on your life.

Peter Wolfing

1. Trying to do everything yourself

Would you look at this and give me your opinion? How many times have you heard that? Here's my answer...

Ask yourself "How much is my time worth? How much is my hourly rate?" Don't know? Here's how to figure it out...

Take how much you want to earn a year and divide by 2000 (average hours worked a year) to get your hourly rate. If you want to make $100,000 a year, your hourly rate is $50 per hour etc.

This was my reply to the person that asked me to look at something...

"It would be too expensive for me to spend 30 minutes of my time to look at it. Nothing personal, just dollars and sense. If I took all the time people asked me for my opinion or to look at something and added it together, it would take a week of my time a year which would cost me 5 figures (or $2000 in the hourly rate example above).

Looking at it this way... It's no big deal. 5 minutes or 10 minutes here or there but over a year, it's turns out to be a week."

Another response could be, "Send me $25 for 30 minutes of my time to look at it". That will certainly see how much conviction that have in what they have to offer.

The same goes for outsourcing things like email, social media etc. Is it worth $50 an hour to go through your email or can you hire someone at $5-$10 p/hour to do it while you do $50 p/hour work? See what I mean? Here's the flip side, you actually have to do the work. In other words, as long as you actually do the work and not have a "personal-party-fest" you're golden.

You need to look at your time as income slipping through the hourglass every hour of every day. Five minutes to watch a YouTube video or Facebook posts that turns into 3 hours.

Then you ask yourself why you made $30,000 this year when your goal is $100,000. Look at how you handle your time. It's probably time spent doing unproductive tasks and not working on tasks that deserve your hourly rate.

That's where outsourcing comes in. Hire outsourcers at a fraction of what your time is worth and focus your tasks on high priority tasks that are important for you to do. You can hand off almost any task for others to do. Start out small, get comfortable with who you are working with and gradually increase the work load.

2. Not being committed (giving it a try) No half way (plane taking off)

There is no such thing earning a mediocre income in network marketing or MLM.

If someone says, I would be happy to earn a few hundred bucks a month, they will most likely give halfhearted effort. They don't achieve enough momentum to get to ANY tangible income. You either go all the way, or no way at all.

Allow me to illustrate.

If a plane takes off, it needs a certain momentum to take off. Let's say if we need about 150 miles per hour to take off, you must exceed that speed or else we are not flying anywhere. It won't take off at 140, 145 or even 149!

Just like in network marketing, only by producing top-notch effort, will outstanding results (often better than their expectation) occur.

3. Trying to understand everything before working

If you are new in your business and you sit down for days (some even take weeks before they make their first phone call) trying out the product, reading all the company brochures, understanding every single calculation about the compensation plan, memorizing all the names of the management in the company (I think we get the idea) …

This is a VERY SLOW way to get started in your business.

Your business is like riding a bike

(1) You don't learn to ride by reading the best manual on riding
(2) You don't learn until the moment you start peddling
(3) You learn by falling down
(4) You also learn how not to fall down after falling down the first time

Reading every single book in the industry

Most MLMs recommend a reading list and they are very helpful for new people especially if the information is factual and informative about the industry. Reading is also a very good habit to develop. But one of the major mistakes of new people is thinking that the more books they read, the more money they are going to make! Those books are mostly self-help books or network marketing self-improvement.

Most newbies spend too much time reading books for a number of reasons

1) Overwhelmed by ignorance. Once again, trying to understand everything before going out there
2) Overwhelmed by fear. The paralysis causes them to retreat to their books without meeting people
3) Overwhelmed by frustration. They assume that after reading their first book, if they don't achieve enough success, they get disheartened and feel the need for self-help more! They try another book. If they fail again, they will blame themselves again. Always remember: Books are subjective. It may work for the author but differently for another.

4. Doing the business alone during the first 30 days

Network marketing doesn't care of if you are a CEO, entrepreneur, manager, housewife, college kid or a beggar. If you are new to the business, you start from ZERO.

If you think you can earn a six-figure income in 2 to 5 years' time without following a system, then you are grasping at thin air. There are people in traditional business who do make it within a few years but everybody learns from SOMEBODY and network marketing is no exception.

Here is an example.

There is this one guy who is an experienced businessman. He started in network marketing and wanted to do it his own way. He rented an office, hired a few staff, created a sales team and sent them out after spending a few hundred thousand dollars on capital alone. After 3 months, his business had nothing to show.

What happened? One of the main reasons of his failure was the fact that network marketing is not designed to run this way. His staff or sales team will not be able to duplicate the process.

There are uplines mentors to guide you and they don't cost you any money to ask for help. I would go to them like a sick man would go to a doctor instead of an architect.

You MUST work closely with your upline. 'But, I don't want to bother them. They are so busy with their huge team. They are making huge income. I am not worthy to speak to them' – WRONG! Don't be afraid to call your upline! Don't worship them. They are there to HELP YOU. The fact that they are earning money from your group gives you the RIGHT to request their help!

- Your Upline is NOT your BOSS.
- Good, sincere uplines are always there to help you and guide you (unless they are untrained and really bossy) but the norm is that generally there will be someone who wants you to succeed.
- We are in business for OURSELVES but NOT BY OURSELVES. If your upline calls you, motivates, encourages and helps you, YOU ARE ONE LUCKY PUPPY!
- Uplines are not OUT TO GET YOU, so don't avoid them – if you do it is YOUR LOSS.

SOLUTION

Stay Informed

Stay informed in what's happening in the industry by subscribing to at least one professional Network Marketing journal.

There are many magazines to choose from and many books written on the subject of Network Marketing. As an "expert" in the field you should be able to speak of it in a professional way and be aware of the latest trends and technologies available to you. Think of how impressed your prospects will be when you can quote them the latest statistics. This helps you to build immediate credibility with your prospects. If you expect to make $20,000 per month, think about what other professionals with similar salaries had to endure before they reached that level, a doctor for example—years of medical schools, educational loans and internships! Don't be skimpy on your education.

5. Quitting your job too soon

Network Marketing is a business like any other business. Don't get psyched into thinking that by burning your bridges and giving all you've got for the next 6 months without any financial support is the way to go.

There is this saying that goes, if the only tool I have is a hammer, all my problems will look like nails. In network marketing, ANY form of financial pressure might kill your prospects because you will keep seeing them like money bags before and even after they 'get in'.

It will change your posture when speaking to prospects. You will probably not even know you're doing it.

You should only 'consider' quitting your job when your income in your business matches at least double your current income.

6. Trying to sell versus being a coach or guidance counselor

What you are doing now will be duplicated downline. Most people would agree that 80-90% of the population are not trained sales people.

Most people who CAN'T SELL, SELL things that DOESN'T SOLVE other people's PROBLEMS, to people who DON'T LIKE BEING SOLD, who perceive you as a SLEAZY SALESMAN trying to get into their pockets.

This means that most newbie make the mistake of trying to sell the opportunity to others (who don't like to be recruited or sold to). People are looking for solutions to their problems – therefore pitching the opportunity usually comes across to prospects as a way for the business builders to get their hands into the pockets.

Focus on asking questions to find out what the problems are for the person you are speaking too and then offer your solution to those problems or tell them that you are not a fit. Maybe ever refer them to something else if necessary. It's very empowering when you are just focusing on providing value to someone and not the end result.

The process is what's important. The numbers will take care of themselves in the long run.

7. Begging people to join your business

New distributors get so hard up on recruiting people that they wind up coming across as high-class beggars in suits. They pitch and sell so much that prospects get afraid of them. Some even chase down their prospects.

Always remember that the ball is in your court. They are the one who needs the opportunity and you are HELPING them to realize this. Don't try to convince them. Instead, when you start helping people out of a genuine concern, dealing with their problems, they will be attracted to you and they in turn will ask you for opportunities.

THE HEALTHY DO NOT NEED A DOCTOR – IT IS THE SICK WHO DO!

Everyone is 'sick' in a certain way and they will look for medicine to solve their problems. Ever seen a doctor hard-selling medicine? No, the patients beg the doctor to CURE them. The patients are looking for a solution and the doctor doesn't sell them, he gives advice and prescribes.

Stop being like a BEGGAR!

Don't go, "Come out and listen to my opportunity, I'll buy you a drink." You spend 2 hours explaining to them your opportunity and in the end, they didn't join you. Why?

How do you prescribe medicine to their sickness? First EXPOSE their sickness, generate interest in your 'medicine' and HELP THEM by UNDERSTANDING their needs.

8. Explaining the business all at once (throwing up on people)

It's a process. One form of information is to lead to the next. The purpose of a phone call is to INVITE the prospect to watch, attend, view something else. Once they do that, you follow up, answer some more questions and feed them more information in a different format. If phone calls can close all the deals, no one will need to hold opportunity meetings anymore or rent buildings. People will just sit at home and call people to become millionaires.

Once your intention is very clear that you are just inviting, you will not confuse people by talking about the opportunity, product or plan. Imagine, the other person on the other side will have a chance to say no to you even after you have explained everything for an hour or so and that is one thing you don't want to have.

9. Telling prospects that this is not MLM or network marketing

Most newbies are so afraid or embarrassed when the prospects ask this these dreadful questions:

1) Is this MLM?
2) Is this one of those networking things?
3) Is this one of those pyramids?
4) Are you trying to recruit me into those Direct Selling things?

Most will go, "Err… Um, no its not. Yeah it's MLM but we're not really selling… hello? Hello??"

Ever get those sinking feelings?

Never ever lie to your prospects. It reflects badly on you and people are not stupid. Either tell them up front it IS an MLM or Networking business (we should be proud that we are in a multi-million-dollar industry) or turn the question around by asking, "What do you mean is it MLM, how do you feel about MLM?" Then let him or her tell it as it is. Make the appointment afterwards.

The industry has come a very long way the last 20 years. As of 2016 almost 200 billion dollars in direct sale globally. This is big business.

10. Tricking your friends to an opportunity meeting

Another big mistake: asking your friends or prospects out for a drink then driving them to an opportunity meeting without informing them that it is an opportunity meeting.

You gain nothing by hiding things from your prospects. Be open and proud of what you are doing! You sponsor people using CONFIDENCE, not trickery.

This stems from insecurities of what you are representing. The first thing to do is examine what you represent. Company. Products. Industry. You need to change your beliefs and feel as though what you are offering is a gift.

Offer value to them. It's a discovery process. You ask questions in order to find their needs in order to see if what you offer is a proper fit to solve their needs.

11. Not contacting their warm list

I often hear from new members "I will contact my personal contacts when I am successful" or "I am part of the NFL Club of No Friends Left". My friends and contacts run away when they see me because they feel I am going to show something else to them.

I understand. I get it. However, do you think millionaires struck gold the first time they tried? No way! They tried over and over again continuing through one failure after another until they found their groove. Most failed many times.

It could be the opportunity is not right for you and it could also be that you were not ready to excel yet due to a lack of the right mindset or skillset on your part. The point is this; you can use this to your advantage. Something like, "John, you know I have been in the direct sales business for some time. I have learned allot and have come a long way. I am somewhat of an expert in the industry now and although some past businesses were not right at the time, I've learned from my experiences and I really feel I have found the right one. Would you do me the courtesy to watch this video?" This is just a suggestion of course.

I've always looked at it as a "moral imperative" to tell people because I just want them to understand what I have to offer. If they can understand it and say it's not for them, I can live with that. But to never tell them... That's something that is unacceptable.

When I first got started in the business, I treated everyone I met as if they had dollar signs on them because I thought that's what was in it for me. Yes, I made money but I was struggling to make money.

It wasn't until my change in thinking that my entire career in network marketing turned around.

I started to think of every person that I talked to as a real person with real lives, families, dreams and goals. I started to think of how I can help them to be able to achieve their goals.

These are real people and real families who will be going into a business with me. For much more than just a few months. Possibly a lifetime.

Not until your contacts are considered the "list of those families whom you will help" rather than "the prospects of whom I can make money from" will your business take off. Once they see that you REALLY CARE and will fight for them will they be interested in what you have to say."

It's not just semantics; it's an entirely different philosophy, mindset and emotional approach to every conversation and human interaction.

This is serious. I just gave you a million-dollar concept.

This is not just lip service guys. Live it. Breath it.

Watch how lives change... including yours.

Don't treat people like targets, capital, pawns or even prospects or just customers.

Treat people like people… people with real desires, fears, hopes, wishes, worries, dreams and ambitions… just like you.

12. Not being yourself

This is the worst kind of disease among distributors.

Imagine if you are looking for your good buddy whom you have known since high school. Every time you see him, all you talk is jive, or nonsense. All of a sudden, you go, "Dude, I've got this business opportunity that will CHANGE YOUR LIFE!" Your friend will think you are on drugs or something.

BE YOURSELF! Don't try being someone you are not.

People don't buy the product or business right away. You are selling you. Be authentic, genuine and caring to them.

13. Telling everyone what their income is

I wouldn't answer this question at all. Why would anyone go around telling others how much money they are making in their JOB? Would you find it insulting if someone asks you what your income is in your business?

If people realize the audacity about asking one's salary in work or business, shouldn't the same apply in network marketing as well?

Most networkers usually go around trying to prove their worth to others so they hope by parading how much (or how little) they are making, they hope to 'gain' others. A successful networker radiates leadership and confidence so most people won't ask them how much they are making. It's all about posture.

Besides, what difference does it make how much money you make. People make money in our industry based on their own efforts and can certainly make more than the person that introduced them.

14. Never calling upline or sponsor, company or upline for help

Business duplicates. If you don't call your upline, do you think your downlines will call you? Do you think it is easier to call ONE upline or having to chase after 10 downlines? 10 might become 100 and you will have a heck of a headache if you do develop the habit to call your upline.

Uplines would be happy to receive your calls because it means business is growing for them and for you as well.

SOLUTION

Have belief in your UPLINE.

Why is this important? Support and training is very important to the development of your business. In network marketing, you are in business for yourself but not by yourself. On the other hand, don't forget that this is your business, and should be treated as such. You must be accountable for your actions. If you succeed, it's the person in the mirror that you should thank. If you do not achieve your goals, you must also look in that same mirror and evaluate honestly what you've done to work towards those goals. Your upline is there to help but they can't do it for you.

Belief in Your Chosen COMPANY.

You must have a solid belief that your program is working in your best interest. This will develop over time as you interact with the staff and attend training's and other functions.

Belief in the PRODUCTS.

The product/s that your company has are quality and appeal to the masses. Regardless if you sell digital products, services or physical products, you need to use them yourself in order to speak truthfully about them. You need to "feel them in your bones".

If you don't really believe in any of these, what does that say about yourself or what you are representing?

15. Not being emotionally detached while prospecting

Don't get too hard up when a prospect says NO to your business. It is easier said than done but we must realize that MLM is just like any business – mixing emotions with it is a recipe for disaster.

When a prospect says NO, we must not take it personally because most of the time they are saying no to the opportunity and not YOU. They might not believe in themselves or they might be having things on their mind at this point of time. They might say YES in the future so don't dissolve friendships just because they don't join you.

The worst thing can happen is that you start feeling sorry for yourself and brood or complain about the business. If you let the NO's sap your excitement, it creates a domino effect which will kill your business for good.

Detach yourself from rejection. It's just part of the process. Thus, focusing on the process and not the instant outcome is the key. That will take care of itself.

16. Not using the products or needing to use the product before selling it

One of the favorite excuses of lazy distributors is, "I haven't tried the product yet therefore I can't start my business yet!"

It is good to use your own product so you can have good testimonials or are convinced yourself. However, have you ever seen a man sell shoes to a lady? If you are selling a good product, its quality will speak for itself, especially when there is a demand (like lady's shoes. Do you think the lady will ask the sales man if he has tried the 'product' before?)

Get as much genuine enthusiasm for the products as you can. It may not be practical to use all the products. Your company may have dozens or hundreds. But diving in and getting a good feel for them is key.

17. Passing negativity downline

When I was a noncommissioned officer in the USMC one of the first rules taught to us as to never pass negativity to those of a lesser rank. Under no circumstances. Leaders in our industry should also not make this mistake.

I don't care if you had a really bad day or your downline is your best friend since junior high. When people join a business, they don't join an opportunity, they join YOU! It means they believe in you and see you as some kind of leader. If you pass negative down, they will lose their confidence in you and your business will be destroyed when they do the same to THEIR downline.

When you have negative or challenges, BRING IT UPLINE. Never down.

18. Reinventing the Wheel

Many seasoned networkers make the mistake of reinventing the wheel. If your company has been established for many years or has even tapped the international market, it is crucial you follow their system as it is in line with the company's direction and is a time-tested business building system.

Don't reinvent the wheel. If you do, your downline may not duplicate and it will spell trouble!

Network marketing has been around for decades. Even newly startups can benefit from the experience of other companies. True some things have changed over time due to technology but the essentials are still the same.

Here's the rule of thumb. Use what others are using that are where you want to be. Once you get there, only then can you decide to do your own thing. This will save you lots of paid and time.

19. I won't give up versus the definition of insanity

It is very important not to give up. But on the other hand, what are they doing about it? The definition of insanity is DOING THE SAME THING OVER AND OVER AGAIN EXPECTING DIFFERENT RESULTS!

There is downline who just refuse to make a change in their lives to get to their goals. They change too slowly and keep doing the same things over and over again. If I didn't have a conscience, I can keep on telling him, "Don't worry, you are doing good. Don't pressure yourself. You are getting there, don't give up and keep on keeping on…" in an effort to keep the numbers up in my organization, or I could tell him the truth and say, "Look, you're not making money here, either you shape up or shape out. We have no room in our team for people not willing to change." Having numbers means squat if your people are not making money and are not growing.

Every so often you need to raise you head up, take a breath and look at your results. You may have to tweak your approach once in a while to get back on course. Adjustments are critical. Learn with each day. Ask yourself what went well and what didn't go well. Then adjust and try again. Constant improvement in this way is the solution to cycle of insanity.

20. If I scratch your back, will you scratch mine?

What if your colleague or associate who is in another MLM asks you to join them? There are times when people get so desperate for business, they go to other opportunity meetings of other companies in an attempt to recruit new blood. This is a good way to expand your network, but... most people will pitch their opportunity to you and will only oblige you mostly in an attempt to gain your friendship and recruit you instead.

The worst thing that can happen is spending a lot of money on joining fees of other companies and not getting a single one of them in yours.

You may scratch someone else's back, but they will not necessarily scratch yours. Don't play tug-of-war.

I have tried this many times back in the day and in every case it was a waste of my time.

21. Placing people under people in an effort to motivate (giving personal sales away/team building)

Some people make promises to other people in order to get them to join. They might say something along the lines of, "If you join under my team, I will build one leg or one group for you!" or they will even place people that they personally recruit under their lazy downline in an effort to motivate them! The rle is that people generally don't value what they have not bought or worked for.

This kind of action not only breeds laziness and dependency, it even slows down their progress! Their other downlines under their group will also expect them to place people under them duplicating a hollow organization.

Even if you are in compensation plan that promotes some sort of spillover, certain expectations should be communicated clearly to downline that spillover will only occur if they meet certain conditions and not let them wait for their uplines for spill over (see my first book on the section marketing plans).

22. Not keeping the business simple

Seasoned networkers might be in MLM for a long time and may even memorize the compensation plan much better than the company themselves!

You may understand the plan but a new prospect might get too confused if you give them information overload!

Normally, for a new distributor, things must be kept so simple for them that they will believe that anybody can do this business! If you bog them down with so many details, they will sit down and think too much.

What to keep in mind is that simplicity kills momentum? Momentum and duplication are only maximized when simple tasks are done with a large group of people over an extended period of time.

If this isn't or can't happen with the methods used, it should not be used on a wide scale.

Too much analysis will lead to paralysis of the mind.

Remember: A downline's effectiveness is only half of yours. If what you are doing cannot be easily duplicated, it does worse down the downline.

23. Trying to turn ducks into eagles

What do ducks do? They quack. What do eagles do? They soar.

What happens when you try to make a duck soar? They fall flat on the ground and they quack louder!

Sad to say, not all downline are like eagles. We wish they are but many people spend too much time with ducks and try to turn them into eagles. They quack too much and everyone becomes ducks in the end (like quaking about the problems in the company, spreading negative all around).

Personally, I would rather have eagles in my team so all of us can soar together.

Now here is the flip side. Never pre-judge a person. Just because they can't start out at the maximum, it's doesn't mean they don't have potential. They may be an eagle chick and have not moulted yet. Keep feeding them, nurturing them and sometimes the baby feathers come off and they soar like nothing you've ever seen. Recognizing the difference is a lost art form and can only be gained through experience.

24. Not setting goals

Make a written plan with all your goals and steps to get there.

Psychologists tell us that when we write something down we are more likely to commit to it. That's why you are required in a contract to place your signature on the dotted line—helps you keep your end of the bargain.

Every business owner should have a goal to which they are aspiring. If you aim for nothing you are likely to strike it. If your plan is to get to a recurring income of $10,000 per month then you should set smaller goals on your way there. Say, $3,000 per month after the first year, then $7,000 per month after the second year and finally $10,000 per month by the third year.

A very important part of writing out this plan is to calculate what is required to get to your goal. So, if you must call 20 people to get 1 'yes', and that prospect is worth $50 per month to you, you will know how many calls you have to make per month to get to $3,000 per month in one year. Looks simple, but most people don't do this kind of calculation and so they run their businesses with blind expectations.

Knowing where you are going is one of the easiest ways to get there!

25. Paying for people to join

Some eager members beg people to join their business and even go so far as to tell them they will even pay the fee to join. This all stems from lack of confidence and belief in the business you are in. People don't value what they don't pay for.

99% of the time it's a waste of your money and time as well as theirs. I've had many people tell me they will "pay my way in" but I don't accept for many reasons. Once of which is that I know human nature. If I were to join, I would rather pay. I even made my son pay just like everyone else. This way he valued the work and effort he put in to get his results.

26. Focusing on what to say rather than posture, belief and attitude.

I am sure you've hear that only a small fraction of how we communicate is verbal. Most comes through loud and clear through or actions both physically and otherwise.

It's the mental aspects that will make or break your success.

55% of all of our communication (that is how we present ourselves to the world) is not what we say and do. It is our body language. It is what we do with our face and our tone. The words you say are a side note. And so, it is essential to believe in yourself each day before you ever set foot online thinking you're going to make a million because - heck – if you don't believe it and you are not congruent... not one customer is going to believe that you're the one to solve all their problems either. So, next time you say 'I don't want to sell myself' or 'I'm not sure people will like my product' or 'Am I charging/asking too much?', make sure that the answer to that is in line with how much you value yourself. Be the value and people will pick up on it. Tell yourself you have lots to offer and that you can do it.

And why not... we talk to ourselves negatively all day long. Add to that, we get pounded by negative news from all directions 24/7... not exactly a great strategy for motivation, is it?

I'll say it one last time… you want to succeed. Do it from the inside out- believe you can first. Believe you are worth that money. It is from a place of fear and worry that most people never pick up that phone and call when they should, most people never ask for what they want (at the price they want) when they know they should. That's what separates the people that do things from the people who just dream about them. You've got to act. You've got to be willing to fail. You've got to be willing to crash and burn. And when it is all done and it's time to get up, it's not your legs that will lift you… it'll be your self-belief.

Deep breath and say it - You're worth it.

27. Building multiple MLM companies at once

There are many schools of thought on this. I was asked by a customer of mine for some advice. The common theme in her email was "Overwhelm, no time and I can't seem to make decent money".

She asked, "If you have any advice you could give me that would simplify things a little, I'd really appreciate it as I have so much going on but my time is limited." After further prodding, I found that she was in 5 deals!

This was my advice...

Focus and simplify. I know it's hard. I fight with that too as I am sure most do. Turn things down. The measure of success is NOT how many things you can do but how many things you say "NO" too.

That's the MASTER SKILL! Saying "No", 99 time out of 100 is the key to success. Chasing the "shiny object" all the time is a sure path to mediocrity.

My rule of thumb is that new people to the industry should focus on one thing. Only when you have sufficient momentum and income should you even consider anything else. So many do the "Portfolio Method" where they have many deals to offer people. This is a sure way to make mediocre money in a few things rather than creating massive momentum on one.

It's a major problem in society right now. We're hit in so many directions with social media, texts, emails, phone calls, new biz opps, TV etc. etc. etc. It's not a lack of information that's the problem. It's lack of a filter to sort it all out and focusing on key tasks that get us to our goals.

I get asked daily to JV for this, join that, come on board here, just join and I will promote for you. It's tough to say "No" because so many seem like great ideas or products.

People jump from one biz opp to another like a fruit fly with only 24 hours to live and never give it time to mature. Hey, I am all for multiple streams of income. I have many. Just give it a chance.

28. Company hopping (MLM junkie)

I would only join serious networkers who work hard in his company. Some MLM junkies are only in for the fast money and you will find it hard to locate your sponsor if he suddenly jumps off towards the next smoking hot opportunity.

Normally, an MLM junkie will join a company after he or she gets really hyped up by the opportunity meeting or rally. They will be on fire for a while before they lose steam and die a natural death. The root cause of the problem would be running into difficulties in their business and when they can't handle the struggles, they find reasons to leave and join other companies because they are 'better' or because their upline 'is better.

Often, we must keep in mind that if we can solve the struggles within ourselves, then we will not find problems with our businesses. The main reason why I would hesitate to join an MLM junkie would be seeing him all hyped up about one opportunity and later on he will tell you to join another one and give reasons why the previous one he got me into is not as good as this one.

Once you find a reputable company be prepared to stay for the long haul.

This goes without saying but if you expect to succeed you must stay the course. The most successful people in life have gone through very trying times but they stuck with it and left a legacy behind. It is often said that tough times don't last but tough people do. The same is true for those seeking to build a solid recurring income. You should commit yourself to at least 3 years before making a decision either way.

Jumping from one opportunity to the next only shows a lack of decision and stability in you planning. Teenagers are expected to fall in and out of love every few months, but married couples have committed for life. Be prepared for a marriage not a fling!

29. Do all the talking and not listening

Continually work to improve your people skills, especially your listening skills.

At its core, Network Marketing is really people management. If you don't like dealing with people, then this is not for you. You are always going to be in direct or indirect contact with people and so you should brush up on your people skills.

One of those skills that you'll need to primarily focus on is your listening skills. One of the most common downfalls of Network Marketers is that they talk too much and don't listen enough. This applies to the majority of salespersons. You have to always take time to listen to the customer because if you do - they will tell you what they are looking for! Here are some quick tips to improve your listening skills (particularly on the telephone):

a) Well ... just stop talking and listen. That's the toughest part.
b) Learn to view things from the prospect's position. Is your prospect a single mom struggling to make ends meet? Empathize and provide the solution.
c) Restate what the person tells you to be sure that you understand what they are saying. This also makes the other person feel "heard."
d) Try not to interrupt them while they are talking—another hard one.

e) Ask a lot of questions for clarification but not to be confrontational.
f) Avoid jumping to unnecessary conclusions and learn to "listen between the lines."
g) Smile! You'll be surprised to see what this does to your tone of voice.

30. Using too much "hype" and overselling it

This business is fine the way it is. No need to over embellish it at all. Doing it this way also tends to attract the type of person that jumps from deal to deal looking for the money. You can build a much more long-term business rather than a house of cards if you recruit based on other factors than money.

31. Not attending events

People are like electric cars. They need to be recharged often. In the age of technology, we tend to be isolated behind a computer or cell phone and although they have many perks, people are still beings that need to socialize.

Have you ever gone to a concert and the moment you enter that stadium, you feel the energy? This is the same in our business. You need to get on calls, trainings and live company events. It's nonnegotiable.

If you are in an office environment, why is the lunch room and water cooler some of the most popular areas of the office. it's the socialization.

People don't necessarily quit. They fade away. Mainly due to this reason.

32. Not targeting the right people

On a scale of 1-10, rate yourself as far as where you would be in a scale of influence.

Let's say you picked that you are a six.

The right people means that you should go after people you feel are 7-8-9-10 on your list.

These are people that have influence and can make your business soar.

Most people are intimidated by people higher than them on the social or economic scale so they recruit lower than them. While I am not here to judge people, an observation and also dare I say a personal one is that I often would try to only prospect people who I was trying to "help" and were less threatening.

So much time is wasted doing this.

Why not target other network marketers?

This may seem to go against the issue of not jumping from opportunity to opportunity, but it is much easier to work with someone who has already worked in the industry than a totally new person. There are list brokers who specialize in mailing list of distributors from companies that have closed down. For these individuals, you don't have to teach them to fish, they already know, and that can be a plus.

In addition to this, you can expect that if they join forces with you they can bring their entire down line from the old company. Of course, one challenge is that these seasoned marketers will also be more difficult to recruit since they will take a more critical stance of your opportunity.

Why not target business-minded people and entrepreneurs?

Here again you are targeting people who are already motivated and understand what it takes to run a successful business. These individuals would also already be networking in their businesses and therefore would be in a position of influence. Such people include chiropractors, real estate agents, sales people and internet marketers. These professionals come in contact with a large number of people and could be the boost that the organization needs. The more 'business minded' your prospects are the more likely you will recruit them.

33. Not telling your story

Your story should be told every chance you get. It's what will be the connector to people as you speak to them. 60 seconds. "Let me tell you my story".

it's a simple 4-part process.

1. Tell your background
2. Talk about the pain you have in your situation
3. How you solved it with your opportunity
4. How bright the future looks

Be real. Be authentic. Really open up to the person. The more you open up to them, they more authentic you are and they will resonate with you.

34. Starting slow and not fast

This business is built easier fast than slow. Getting momentum is like an airplane trying to take off. You need to reach a specific speed on the runway in order to gain flight. Unless the proper thrust is applied, there is no way you will take off.

Once that thrust is applied and you become airborne, flight becomes much easier and even less fuel is need to maintain flight. You can even cruise for parts of the flight.

So many say they are going to put in 5-10 hours a week in their business. While this is ok, they will likely not get airborne.

35. Not preparing your new recruits

When I was in boot camp it was an extreme experience. For 13 weeks, we did everything imaginable to prepare us just in case we went to the battlefield. Ever wonder why you see troops running to the danger? It's because they were trained to face the fear and inevitable stress.

In our business, it's the same. As a leader, you must prepare your members for the inevitable naysayers, dream stealers, rejection and stresses of the industry ahead of time. When you do this and they go out into the world and start their business, when someone says something negative, they will be prepared and think to themselves "You know, Peter told me you would say that! That's funny.". Without doing that, the same instance will be like a nuclear bomb for their confidence and most never recover.

36. Have unrealistic expectations about income

I think many of us fall into this due to the nature of the business. It's so easy to be seduced by the sirens call of quick money, cars, yachts, time freedom and you can do it with little effort. It's very seductive.

Thus, when many join, if they are recruited in this way, they expect way too much in income without the appropriate effort to make it happen. There is a disconnect.

When a traditional business is purchased and documents signed, people are told "It's hard. Really hard. You may even lose all your money and more". Yet they think, "That sounds reasonable".

Yet in our industry somehow people thing money falls out of the sky. It's the "Do nothing and make money" mentality. I agree that our industry is fantastic and the best business model out there. It's not perfect but neither is anything else. It's more efficient and really doesn't need to be sold to people that way. it sets them up for failure by expecting unrealistic goals.

37. Quitting too soon

We've heard stories so many times of people quitting just before the vein of gold was found by the next person. The same here as well. As long as you are learning daily, improving your skills, and growing, you will do well. However, if you continue to do unsuccessful habits, it's going to be really difficult and you will probably fail.

Your resolve to continue through the face of the ups and downs maintaining your passion is key.

38. Relying on a system or technology to do all the work for you

The magic system is going to do it for me. Everyone wants a short-cut to success. Dreams are free but many just don't want to pay the price to achieve them.

It seems in the technology age; people are becoming more and more stunted in the personal communication and relationship building area. We hide behind PC's, cell phones and more and are just afraid to open up and talk to people.

Don't get me wrong. I love technology to sort and sift. It's like prospecting using a backhoe rather than a shovel. However, you still have to have that connection and actually speak to people.

39. Not actually talking to people

This is where most blow it. They don't call leads back and hope they join by some whips of magic.

Becoming skilled at talking to people and following up with leads is one skill that will put you in the top of the leaderboard. People don't bite yet it seems incredibly difficult for most to pick up the phone.

Why not start small and work your way into it by doing 3 way calls with s sponsor or upline that is more seasoned in this area. The gradually start to do the call yourself with them as support. A service called www.hyperdialer.com is great for this because it has what they call a "whisper function". This is where your coach or upline is on the phone with you but the prospect can't hear them. it's a fantastic function to get you rolling.

40. Not treating yourself as an entrepreneur

We are trained from the moment we are born to be a worker and be an employee by getting the skills to work for someone else thus making someone else's dreams come true. They go to grade school and maybe college and all the while doing the same. Throughout this process we are in a structure that tells us what to do and evaluated, grades and even punishes if not done. We are told when to go on breaks, vacations and more.

Contrast that to when we are an entrepreneur, all of a sudden we are free... or so we thought. We join a network marketing company and no one is over us telling us what to do. It's totally self-motivated. People often can't handle this freedom and run back to the structure they know.

The way to overcome this is to treat yourself as employee. You are both the boss and employee. Don't let yourself get away with anything. Good news is you can fire yourself and hire yourself right back.

41. Spending more than you can sustain

If you are a leader with a large group of downline in different states around the country, you could exhaust yourself doing meetings and rallies everywhere. You may be making 5 figures, but always be careful.

Once, there is this leader who had people in another state asking him to do a rally in their town. He rented this hotel for a few thousand dollars. His people promised that they will bring more than 50 new prospects. But when the actual day came, only 5 turned up and only 1 signed up. The trip was a total disaster and cost him a bomb!

Another big mistake is spending all the money you earned on new cars and houses. But what happens if your network is not stable? There may be many leaders under your team but you will never know what happens the next day. Leaders can join other companies; they might get sick or even die! Then how are you going to pay for your new house, car or that new yacht you bought? Never spend too much. Always save for a rainy day.

42. Leaving newly sponsored members to fend for themselves

Of course not. The funny thing is, new downlines are like newborn babies! Hard to imagine, huh? I am not trying to insult anyone here, but there is a high dropout rate for newcomers and it is scary. Why does this happen?

A newborn baby if not taken care of will be a target of germs (negative energy, rejection, feeling emotionally down in the business), kidnapping (head-hunted by other companies without armed with the right information), and will cry a lot (they will whine to the upline when problems come). I have seen corporate businessmen whine like little children when they didn't get their commission on time or the admin never replied their e-mails or even when their friends said something negative.

Downlines require your attention especially in the first few months where they are most vulnerable.

43. Not Driving the Lines Deep

This means going deeper and deeper into your group to find the "Hot Molecules". If you find someone on your third or fourth level that "sees" the business, work with them as if you personally sponsored them. This will help "lock in" those above them and will keep them in the business because they will be making money. There is a saying that goes, "It's harder to leave when you have children". That's true in life as in this business.

WIDTH VS. DEPTH: Usually the school of thought is to go 3 to 5 people wide and work deep until they are "locked in". When someone has 3 to 4 people under them, they are more likely to stay in the business. Then work with your next 3 to 5 people. You need to support and work with them until they have learned to duplicate your efforts. Help show them success as fast as possible.

44. No such thing as total retirement

Contrary to popular belief, there is no such thing as total retirement in network marketing.

If you stop building at the deepest levels of your organization, they might start dying off one by one. The attrition will follow its way up until even your leaders might quit themselves (out of frustration or loss of income) and you will be the only one left.

Even people who have built groups of thousands can lose them overnight if they are not careful. Unstable companies or change of management can happen but with sound leadership, your people will follow you no matter which company you go to. Just make sure you take care of your leaders and especially all you new people. You can't just leave the fate of your babies to your other slightly older babies.

Your MLM business is your business and your responsibility to get your group moving.

45. Mishandling of rejection.

This is a big one.

When someone is first introduced to the concept of Network Marketing they become very motivated—mainly by the income possibilities—to start recruiting right away. Most companies will teach you to start with a list of your warm market and work from there. Even though this is a logical route, rejection from this group can be very discouraging and most people stop there. This means that the majority of recruits will give up after speaking with their spouses for example.

Only lately has Network Marketing become recognized as a viable and respected profession and many are still quick to cry, "Oh! You mean a pyramid scheme". This comes because of the negative press that many famous companies have received and the general misunderstanding of the public.

The more you get rejected (failure) and learn from your efforts, the closer you will align yourself with success. You can't have success without failure. If someone tells you NO; you are closer to a YES!

Perseverance, Tenacity, Consistency and Endurance will get you to the millionaire mindset.

You can't help but succeed if you keep trying. If it was only skill, I would not have succeeded. It's about challenging yourself to keep trying. Keep marketing. Keep talking to people and sharing your business.

This business is not for everyone.

That's ok. It's ok when people tell you "No".

You need to think different about rejection. Some people take rejection personally and it destroys them.

If you think rejection means... you have no value, no worth, stupid, bad decision, not likeable, if you believe that it will be your reality then you need to overcome that fast!

Rejection is just a sorting mechanism on who's open and who's closed, who's ready and who's not.

You are liberating people and giving them options compared to something they may currently be doing that may not suit them as well.

People offer you the gift on "NO" to let you know where to spend your time.

If you also think that what you're doing is to give value to people and you ask them questions to see if what you have to offer is a solution to their problem.

Retrain your mind and think differently regarding rejection. Get proud when someone rejects you.

Fail as much as possible and as quick as possible.

Be prepared to handle rejection.

Who said that any kind of selling was easy? But it all comes down to attitude. If you can understand that a rejection of the opportunity that you are so excited about is not a rejection of you as a person, then you are on your way. "No" must be interpreted as "next". This is easier said than done but it's the price of success. The Internet and other new technologies now allow some rejection proof approaches, such as using lead capture pages and autoresponder messages. These methods serve to "pre-qualify" your prospects.

Part of preparing your mind for these 'negative' people is to fill your mind with positive messages. There are many Network Marketing and "positive thinking" speakers that will help you keep your spirits up. You will be surprised to discover the boost that motivational tapes and books can give to your attitude in general. This is one of the benefits of being in this industry—it teaches you to have a brighter outlook on life.

REJECTION AND ATTRITION IS PART OF THE BUSINESS: Remember the 80/20 rule. You will find that about 20% of the people you sponsor will dig down deep and go for it! Just like in any business.

46. False expectations for too early results with too little effort.

Depending on the way in which the business is presented, one can get the impression that there is not much effort involved. I mean, just get two who gets two and you can become rich. When early recruits realize that considerable networking and marketing is involved in Network Marketing, disappointment quickly sets in. There is work involved, and any business that presents a plan to you and says that you don't have to do anything is peddling a lie. All successful network marketers worked for their success.

Many marketers do not factor into their planning the cost of advertising their business. This cost can eat up a good chunk of your investment especially when you are just launching. The idea here is that you have to regard this as a normal business and not just a trial run venture.

Be realistic in your expectations.

To expect too much too soon will only set you up for a possible let down. Accept that this is a legitimate business that requires investment of time and effort and you must be prepared to sow the seeds for the harvest you expect to reap. Who builds a house without first considering the cost?

When you are quoted the salaries of the big recruiters, be sure to ask how much time and money they spent to get to that level. This information will give you a clearer picture.

47. Lack of focus.

Network marketers have gained a reputation of jumping around and changing companies like they change clothing. At least this applies to those who flirt with success but never reach it.

As I mentioned before, those who survive the early years normally go on to do very well. However, there are many people who are looking for the 'next big thing' and keep jumping from opportunity to opportunity. This normally describes the behavior of those in search of the ever evasive 'ground-floor opportunity'. The rule of thumb here is that you should establish yourself in one solid company before venturing off into other companies. And if you do work more than one opportunity, make them complementary to each other. A perfect example is working a leads company which you'll need anyway to feed your primary Network Marketing company. In fact, if you find any tools that enhances your business, why not purchase from a company that has a compensation plan attached?

48. Failure to work an easily duplicable marketing plan.

With the advent of the Internet and all the new communication means that it affords, Network Marketing has come a long way from the home meetings and house to house presentations. Doing these presentations was very intimidating to many people and so the recruiting chain often broke along the way. The key here is that if the recruiting machine does not have a system that anyone can comfortably do, it will come to a screeching halt. Good trainers know that a simple system must be in place or the trainer's efforts will not be properly duplicated. If the impression is given that a recruit must be turned into an instant public speaker, giving motivational speeches at the local Hilton, they can be easily scared off.

At the same time, you must take the time to learn the system and become familiar enough with the products that you can tell a friend about its benefit. As a user, yourself, this should not be difficult. A caution here is to work the system that has been field tested, rather than trying to invent your own methods. This doesn't mean that you shouldn't be innovative, but there is no use to reinvent the wheel either, so be teachable.

Do not make the business more complicated than it needs to be.

Stick with what works.

There is always the temptation to improve on the methods that experienced networkers have shown to work. Go with what works, not with what should work. If you find a system that has been working just plug into it and squeeze the last drop of success you can get from this. This means that you must show yourself teachable to your up line and be willing to teach your down line members the same system. Success normally comes from doing what works over and over again until it becomes second nature.

Another note of caution is that you should not expect from your recruits what you are not doing yourself. There many networkers who will give advice that they are not willing to follow. In other words, they get their team members to "do the dirty work" for them. This practice takes away from the real meaning of duplication—I'm doing the same thing that I'm teaching you to do.

49. Baby-sitting of downline members.

Teaching is surely a part of the game of building a strong team. Some marketers make the mistake of doing too much for their down line members thinking that if they didn't their recruits will leave. This often backfires, however, because the down line members become comfortable and depend too heavily on their up line and never grow strong enough to build their own teams. There is only so much you can do for someone and no more. These spoiled over-dependent down line members can become a liability instead of an asset to your team. So avoid the temptation to micromanage your team; you'll get burnt out. Teach your team members to fish instead of fishing for them.

Train and then let loose!

The real power of Network Marketing is the power of leverage. Rather than using 100% of your own effort, you are using 1% of the effort of a hundred. If your down line members become too dependent upon you then they will be using 110% of your effort. This can easily lead to rapid burnout.

So the key here is to train your frontline members, then train them to train their frontline members. As you gain leadership experience in the business then you can occasionally pick up the slack for a colleague. The important thing here is that your team members understand that effort is required on their part or they cannot expect your support.

Here are some additional insider tips on really hitting the ground running. These 'secrets' are learned from the study of those who have made millions in this industry.

50. Going into Management Mode

A leader that spends all his time managing their distributors and very little time building their own lines. This is a trap that many people fall into. You should have a balance of sponsoring, teaching and going deep.

Let's wrap it up...

Success is usually inconvenient.

As you can surmise from reading this book, your journey is full of potential potholes that can derail your business.

Examine the achievements of successful network marketers and you will find that they have paid a price that is in direct proportion to the amount of success they have earned. Rarely do you have the "accidental top earner". Did you realize that many "overnight successes" labored in obscurity for many years before they were made it?

If you look closer, you will uncover consistent effort, day in and day out as well as massive rejection to get the success that has been achieved. One major key to get to the top faster is to get rejected as fast as you can, as often as you can, as massively as you can!

Rejection is uncomfortable. Success is inconvenient. Does it stand to reason that this is the reason why there is so much room at the top? That's exactly why. People are creatures of comfort and habit. They go to where it's comfortable because anything that rubs them the wrong way, repels them like oil in water!

Nothing worthwhile ever comes easily. You chose this wonderful industry we are in for a reason. When you factor in the investment and risk involved, network marketing gives us all the opportunity to reach stellar heights that are totally unobtainable elsewhere. You need to also understand that it's a business and will pay you like one or it will be an expensive hobby.

As you consider what you want to achieve, ask yourself if you are willing to sacrifice for what you expect to receive. You need to be mentally prepared to the realization of the sacrifices you will need to give to get the goal you want to accomplish. Know also that at the beginning you will do allot of work that you will not get paid for so that later you will get paid for allot of work you don't do!

Burn that in your brain. I am not here to scare you to not take action. If I had that result then you are not ready and I probably saved you lots of time, money and stress. It is meant to prepare you for what it takes to get to the top. I will tell you from first-hand experience that it's not crowded. There's plenty of room up here. Come join the party. Everyone is welcome... if they are willing to pay the price.

Peter Wolfing